English monarchs had used **burning at the stake** to punish heretics the 1400s, but none used it quite as much as Mary. It was an agonisi slow death, during which victims could feel, see and smell their flesh right before their eyes, suffering up to an hour of torturous pain bef they died. Some witnesses reported seeing victims' blood boiling an steam bursting through the veins of their bodies.

In all, Mary had 283 Protestants burned at the stake, including 56 women, in five years. The most famous victim was Thomas Cranmer, the former Archbishop of Canterbury. Cranmer was England's leading Protestant and had masterminded Henry VIII's divorce from Mary's mother, Catherine of Aragon. This had made Mary's teenage years a misery. Even though Cranmer renounced his Protestant faith six times, Mary still had him burned.

Mary suffered a number of miscarriages, and failed to have a child. Her husband Philip abandoned her and returned to Spain. On 17 November 1558, Mary died. To her Catholic supporters, she was remembered as 'Mary the Pious', but to her Protestant opponents she would always be remembered as 'Bloody' Mary.

Illustration of William Sautre being burned at the stake for heresy

Foxe's Book of Martyrs

John Foxe was a Protestant cleric who fled to Switzerland during Mary's reign. He wrote a bestselling account of the period in 1563. It was a powerful work of Protestant **propaganda**, which helped to establish Mary's reputation as 'Bloody'.

The book tells in vivid detail how each Protestant **martyr** died. One account describes the burning at the stake of two bishops, Latimer and Ridley. Friends of the two bishops tied bags of gunpowder around their necks to ensure a quick death, but the wet wood burned too slowly. Latimer was heard calling out to his dying friend, 'We shall this day light such a candle as I trust shall never be put out.'

Execution of the Duke of Suffolk, from Foxe's book

Fact

In the last year of her life, Mary had a pain and a large lump in her stomach. She was convinced it was a child, but it was in fact the tumour that killed her.

Check your understanding

1. How were Mary I's religious views different from those of her half-brother Edward VI?
2. Why did the Wyatt rebellion take place in 1554?
3. Why did Mary I's religious policy become more pro-Catholic, and anti-Protestant, from July 1554 onwards?
4. Why was being 'burned at the stake' such an agonising death?
5. What religious viewpoint was Foxe's Book of Martyrs written to support?

Elizabeth I

In 1558, the throne passed to Mary's steely and independent-minded half-sister, Elizabeth I. She made a series of thoughtful decisions that would ensure the stability of her 44-year reign.

The most pressing issue facing Elizabeth was England's religion. In her lifetime, England had moved away from Catholicism and then back again under her father, much further towards Protestantism under her brother, and then back to Catholicism under her sister. When Elizabeth came to the throne, England was split between those Protestants who wanted to see the Reformation taken further, and those who still had a deep affection for Catholic ceremonies and rituals.

Coronation portrait of Elizabeth I

Elizabeth's religious policy, known as the '**Elizabethan Religious Settlement**', was a masterstroke of compromise. Elizabeth established a Church of England that was Protestant in doctrine, but Catholic in appearance. Cranmer's Book of Common Prayer returned, services were conducted in English, Catholic ceremonies and rituals were banned, and priests were allowed to marry. However, bishops were retained, priests could wear traditional vestments, and church decorations such as stained glass windows were permitted.

At first, Catholics were not forced to convert to Protestantism. Attendance at Protestant services on Sunday was compulsory, but the punishment for not attending was kept low: a fine of 12 pence. Elizabeth was willing to turn a blind eye to Catholics who worshipped in private. As her advisor Sir Francis Bacon explained, she was not interested in creating 'windows into men's souls'.

Marriage

The next challenge was marriage. Elizabeth's Protestant advisors, such as her loyal Secretary of State William Cecil, were desperate for Elizabeth to marry and produce an heir. An endless supply of English noblemen and European princes wanted Elizabeth's hand in marriage, but none was quite right.

Marrying a European royal such as Philip II of Spain or Prince Eric XIV of Sweden would have made England overly attached to a foreign power. Marrying an Englishman such as Robert Dudley, the Earl of Leicester, would have caused jealousy and conflict at home.

Though none of her advisors agreed with her, Elizabeth believed that she could serve England best by providing a long period of stability but no heir. Elizabeth's stubborn determination won out. As she told her court favourite Robert Dudley: "I will have here but one mistress and no master".

Mary Queen of Scots

In 1570, the Pope issued a **Papal Bull** against the 'pretended Queen of England', declaring Elizabeth to be a heretic. It ordered English Catholics not to follow their queen, or risk being expelled from the Catholic Church.

Some English Catholics were driven to plot to kill the Queen, assured that this was the right path in the eyes of God. Elizabeth's government was thrown into panic. The greatest threat to Elizabeth was her Catholic younger cousin, Mary Queen of Scots (not to be confused with her half-sister Mary I). In 1568, Mary Queen of Scots was expelled from Scotland, and sought protection in England. Elizabeth was duty bound to offer shelter to her cousin, but Elizabeth also knew that some Catholics intended to kill her and place Mary Queen of Scots on the throne. So, for years Elizabeth imprisoned her cousin Mary in various **stately homes** and castles across England.

Portrait of Mary Queen of Scots

Elizabeth's government uncovered numerous Catholic plots to kill the queen, including one involving her own court doctor! After years of trying, Elizabeth's chief spymaster Francis Walsingham finally found the evidence he needed to implicate Mary. She had been communicating with a Catholic named Sir Anthony Babington who planned to assassinate Elizabeth I. They used coded letters, smuggled in and out of her prison in a waterproof case at the bottom of barrels, which Walsingham's spies managed to decode. In 1587, after 19 years of imprisonment, Mary Queen of Scots was beheaded.

As more and more plots against her life were uncovered, Elizabeth became increasingly intolerant towards Catholics. Fines for non-attendance at church increased, and in 1585 being a Catholic priest in England was made a crime punishable by death. In all, 180 Catholics were killed during Elizabeth's reign.

Fact

In many stately homes today, you can still see 'priest holes', where Catholic families would hide visiting priests, sometimes for days on end.

Francis Walsingham

Walsingham was Queen Elizabeth's chief 'spymaster', and had a network of spies across Europe. Walsingham would torture captured Catholics for further information. The Catholic priest Edmund Campion had iron spikes driven under his finger and toenails, and was placed on the **rack**. A Catholic from York named Margaret Clitherow was tortured by having a door put on top of her, and heavier and heavier weights were placed on the door until she died.

Check your understanding

1. What aspects of Catholicism did the Protestant Church of England retain under Elizabeth I?
2. Why did Elizabeth I believe neither a foreign nor an English husband would be suitable for her?
3. Why did the 1570 Papal Bull cause Elizabeth I's life to be in further danger?
4. What led to Mary Queen of Scots finally being sentenced to death in 1587?
5. How did Elizabeth I's treatment of Catholics in England change over the course of her reign?

The Elizabethan Golden Age

Due to Elizabeth I's wise decision making, England enjoyed an unprecedented period of peace and stability during her reign.

Art, trade and culture all flourished in England, and this period is sometimes termed the 'Elizabethan **Golden Age**'. Religious plays had been a strong part of the Catholic Church, but they were banned during the English Reformation. As a result, secular theatre became increasingly popular. Wealthy nobles would hire troupes of travelling actors to provide them with entertainment.

The theatre

In 1576, London gained its first public theatre. Built in the London suburb of Shoreditch and called The Theatre, it lay safely outside the city of London, where theatre had been banned. Theatre was very different during the Elizabethan period, with drinks and food sold in the stalls, and plenty of interaction between the actors and the audience. Rowdy audiences would cheer, boo and pelt poor performers with food. Elizabeth I enjoyed the theatre, and the best performances in London's public theatres would be transferred to perform at the royal court.

There were many famous playwrights of this period, but none more so than William Shakespeare. Between 1590 and 1613, he wrote 38 plays including comedies such as *Much Ado About Nothing* and *A Midsummer Night's Dream*, tragedies such as *Hamlet* and *Macbeth*, and histories such as *Henry V* and *Richard III*. Little is known about Shakespeare's life, but he is thought to have gone to a grammar school in Stratford-Upon-Avon, before going to London to work as an actor. Many phrases that we still use today originated with Shakespeare, such as 'vanished into thin air', 'tongue-tied' and 'the game is up'.

One of the few surviving portraits of William Shakespeare

The Elizabethan court

The Queen's favourite noblemen and advisors together made up the royal court. They would stay together in the Queen's various palaces, and enjoy glittering entertainments, such as plays, dancing, jousting, hunting, banqueting and concerts. Elizabeth I liked to surround herself with brilliant and handsome young men, such as Sir Walter Raleigh.

Raleigh was a dashing soldier, who had fought for the Protestants in France (known as Huguenots) during the **Wars of Religion**. He was 6 foot tall, had dark curly hair, and wore a pearl earring in one ear. In 1578, he sailed to the Americas, and returned with a collection of presents for the Queen, including two Native Americans and some potatoes. Raleigh also returned with tobacco, and made smoking a fashionable pastime in Elizabeth's Court. Sir Walter Raleigh entranced Elizabeth with his charm, and many suspected Elizabeth was in love with him. When

Portrait of Sir Walter Raleigh

Elizabeth discovered that Raleigh had secretly married, she flew into a jealous rage and threw him in jail.

During the summer, Elizabeth would embark on her magnificent 'Royal **progresses**', being hosted by members of her royal court across England. Favourites who wanted to impress the Queen spared no expense entertaining her at their stately homes, such as William Cecil's Burghley House.

Gloriana

By 1601, Queen Elizabeth was growing old. She was called to Parliament that year, as many of its members were angry with the high taxes needed to pay for war with Ireland. Elizabeth quelled their anger by delivering what became known as her Golden Speech. It concluded: "And though you have had, and may have, many mightier and wiser princes sitting in this seat, yet you never had, nor shall have, any that will love you better."

Aware that it was probably the last time they would hear their queen speak, the Members of Parliament lined up to kiss Elizabeth's hand as they left, many in tears. Two years later, Elizabeth died. After decades of religious conflict, she brought peace to England. Today, Elizabeth is remembered as one of England's greatest rulers.

Illustration of Queen Elizabeth I in procession with her courtiers

Sir Francis Drake

Francis Drake was the greatest explorer of Elizabethan England. A tough young sailor from Devon, Drake worked for Queen Elizabeth as a '**privateer**', raiding Spanish **galleons** and trade ports in the Americas and returning to England with their cargo.

In an epic journey from 1577 to 1580, Drake became the first Englishman to circumnavigate the globe on his ship the ***Golden Hind***. Having sailed through the treacherous Magellan Strait, Drake captured an unprotected Spanish galleon full of gold off the coast of Peru. When he returned from his voyage, Drake moored the *Golden Hind* in Deptford, and invited the Queen to join him for dinner on board. Elizabeth knighted Francis Drake on board the deck of his own ship.

Fact

In one famous story, Sir Walter Raleigh saved Elizabeth I from walking through a muddy puddle by throwing down his cape so that she could walk over it.

Check your understanding

1. Why did the theatre become increasingly popular during Elizabeth I's reign?

2. How was the theatre different during the Tudor period compared with the theatre today?

3. What were Queen Elizabeth's 'progresses'?

4. In what ways were Sir Walter Raleigh and Sir Francis Drake similar?

5. What did Elizabeth I tell the Members of Parliament during her Golden Speech?

Unit 3: The later Tudors
The Spanish Armada

During Elizabeth I's reign, Philip II of Spain was the most powerful king in Europe. He was a leading defender of Catholicism in the European Wars of Religion.

As a devout Catholic, Philip II had many reasons to dislike England. He had briefly been King of England until the death of Mary I. Philip courted Elizabeth I as his next wife, but Elizabeth rejected Philip's advances. Elizabeth gave English support to Protestant armies fighting in Europe, and she openly ordered English privateers such as Francis Drake to attack and rob Spanish ships of their precious cargo whilst returning from the Americas.

When Elizabeth executed Mary Queen of Scots in 1587, this seemed to guarantee a Protestant future for England. Philip II knew he would have to act fast if England was to return to the old faith.

The Armada

Philip set about building the largest naval invasion force Europe had ever seen. On 28 May 1588, it set sail from Lisbon for England. Named the 'Spanish **Armada**', Philip's force consisted of 130 large ships known as 'galleons', 8000 sailors and 18 000 soldiers. However, it had one crucial weakness: the commander of the fleet, the Duke of Medina Sidonia, had little sailing experience. He even suffered from sea-sickness.

In Holland, the Spanish had a crack-force of 30 000 experienced soldiers under the command of the Duke of Parma. Philip's plan was for the Armada to sail to France where he would meet the Duke of Parma's army, and then invade England. The English navy, under the command of Lord Howard of Effingham and Francis Drake, numbered 200 ships. Though more numerous, their ships were smaller, and had much less gun-power.

After weeks of waiting, the Spanish Armada was sighted off the coast of Cornwall on 19 July. A series of hilltop bonfires called 'signalling towers' were lit. This spread the news towards London and across the south coast: England was under attack.

That evening, the Spanish approached the English fleet moored in Portsmouth. With the wind blowing into the harbour, the English were vulnerable to attack, and the Spanish had their best chance of a quick and easy victory. However, Medina Sidonia wanted to stick to his orders to meet the Duke of Parma in France first, so he sailed straight past the English fleet.

Painting of English and Spanish ships during the Armada, completed shortly after the event

For a week, the English chased the Spanish up the channel, engaging in a few skirmishes. Then, on the 27 July, the Spanish anchored off Calais to pick up their reinforcements. To their shock, the Duke of Parma had not yet arrived. His army of 30 000 men was nowhere to be seen.

English victory

The following evening, on the 28 July, the English devised a tactical masterstroke. They filled eight ships with gunpowder and tar, creating '**hellburners**'. In the middle of the night, these were set on a course for the Spanish ships anchored at Calais. The Spanish commanders awoke to see the burning ships speeding towards them, and panicked. They cut their anchors and were scattered along the channel.

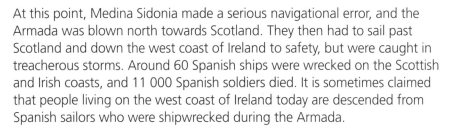

Modern illustration of the English hellburners

As a consequence, the Spanish lost their powerful 'crescent' formation, and were easy to attack. On the 7 August, the two sides met at the Battle of Gravelines, where the smaller English ships sailed rings around the larger Spanish galleons, sinking five and damaging many more.

At this point, Medina Sidonia made a serious navigational error, and the Armada was blown north towards Scotland. They then had to sail past Scotland and down the west coast of Ireland to safety, but were caught in treacherous storms. Around 60 Spanish ships were wrecked on the Scottish and Irish coasts, and 11 000 Spanish soldiers died. It is sometimes claimed that people living on the west coast of Ireland today are descended from Spanish sailors who were shipwrecked during the Armada.

Tilbury speech

The day after the Battle of Gravelines, Elizabeth I visited her troops who were stationed at Tilbury and awaiting the invasion. Dressed in a silver suit of armour, Elizabeth delivered the most famous speech of her reign. In it she declared: *"I know I have the body of a weak and feeble woman; but I have the heart and stomach of a king – and of a King of England too."*

Little did Elizabeth know, the English Royal Navy had already defeated the Spanish Armada. Had they not, Philip II may well have deposed Elizabeth I, and returned England to Catholicism. The history of England could have been very different indeed.

Fact

A year before the Armada, Francis Drake made a first strike on the Spanish fleet harboured in the Spanish port of Cadiz. Drake took them by surprise, sank 30 ships and set fire to the city. He boasted that he had 'singed the King of Spain's beard'.

Check your understanding

1. Why did Philip II of Spain want to invade England?

2. Why was it such a mistake for Medina Sidonia not to attack on the evening of 19th July?

3. Why did the English send 'hellburners' sailing towards the Spanish ships moored in Calais?

4. What happened to the Spanish Armada following the Battle of Gravelines?

5. What message did Elizabeth I deliver to the troops in her Tilbury Speech?

Rich and poor in Tudor England

By the time the Tudors came to power, some of England's most powerful noble families had died out during the Wars of the Roses.

Fewer noblemen meant fewer challenges to the monarchy, and the Tudor monarchs made sure that the nobility remained small and easily managed for the rest of their reigns.

When the Catholic Duke of Norfolk was executed in 1572 for treason, there were no more dukes left in England. By 1600, there was one marquess, 18 earls, two viscounts and 37 barons, making up a class of just 58 noblemen in the whole country. Most significantly, starting with the reign of Henry VII, it was illegal for noblemen to keep private armies. Many swapped their now unnecessary castles for stately homes. Tudor noblemen were still great landowners, but their days as an elite military class were over.

The gentry

The real ruling class of Tudor England was the **gentry**. Numbering around 15 000 families, members of the gentry were landowners without noble titles. Like the nobility, they made enough money from renting their land to tenant farmers to pursue lives of leisure. The gentry had the time to read and socialise, and called themselves 'gentlemen'.

Painting of a fair in Bermondsey, near London, from 1569

The decreasing power of the nobility during the Tudor period made it surprisingly easy for bright men of humble birth to rise to the top of society, as can be seen in the careers of Thomas Wolsey and Thomas Cromwell. Called '**new men**', many of these upwardly mobile Tudors benefited from the Dissolution of the Monasteries. It allowed them to buy church land cheaply and become landowning gentlemen.

The division between the landed wealthy and the working poor were as clear as ever in Tudor England. The medieval Sumptuary Laws remained in place, so only a nobleman could wear gold or silver cloth, and only a lord could wear red or blue velvet. At the other end of the scale, the Wool Cap Act of 1571 stated that all working people over the age of seven had to wear a wool cap on Sundays or holy days.

For the wealthy, fashions in Tudor England were always changing. During the reign of Henry VIII, men wore bulging sleeves and shoulder pads to make their upper body look powerful, along with enlarged codpieces to emphasise their masculinity. Men's fashion became more refined during the reign of Elizabeth I. Men began to wear short padded trousers called

Painting of the diplomat Sir Henry Unton, with a rather large ruff

hose, and a buttoned up jacket known as a **doublet**. From the 1560s onwards, any self-respecting lady or **gentleman** had to wear a **ruff**: an elaborate lace collar encircling the neck, which – as the playwright Ben Johnson observed – created the impression of a head on a plate.

Life for the poor

The population of England grew rapidly during this period, almost doubling from 2.4 million in 1520 to 4.1 million in 1600. This meant there were often not enough jobs to go round, so mass unemployment was common. To make matters worse, England's monasteries – which for centuries had cared for the poor during times of hardship – no longer existed.

Tudor woodcut showing a vagrant being whipped through the streets

As a result, travelling beggars called **vagrants** became a common sight in Tudor towns, and people in Tudor England often spoke of an increase in crime. At first, Tudor governments responded harshly. Begging was made illegal for everyone except the disabled or elderly. Able-bodied vagrants caught begging would have a large hole burnt through their right ear with a hot iron. If they reoffended, vagrants could be imprisoned or even executed.

The government did gradually begin to take more responsibility for the poor. From 1563 onwards, the '**Poor Laws**' were passed, requiring parishes to collect taxes from the local population, to provide help for the poor. The Tudors made a clear distinction between two different types of poor. The **'deserving' poor**, who were unable to work through old age, disability or the lack of jobs, were believed to deserve help. Whereas it was believed the 'undeserving' poor were simply idle, and deserved nothing.

Tudor football

Sport was very popular in Tudor England, in particular football. Aside from being played with a leather ball, there were few similarities with the modern game. Tudor football was often played between villages, with no boundaries to the pitch, and no limit to the number of players on each side. Players could pick up and run with the ball. Fights, broken bones, and even deaths were common.

Fact

Elizabeth I was no exception to the Tudor love of fashion. An inventory of the royal wardrobe in 1600 recorded that she owned 269 gowns, 96 cloaks, and 99 robes.

Check your understanding

1. Why was the nobility weaker during the Tudor period, than in the medieval period?
2. Why were landowners such as the nobility and gentry able to pursue lives of leisure?
3. How did men's fashions change from the reign of Henry VIII, to the reign of Elizabeth I?
4. Why was vagrancy such a problem during the 16th century?
5. What was the difference, according to the Poor Laws, between the deserving and the undeserving poor?

Unit 3: The later Tudors
Knowledge organiser

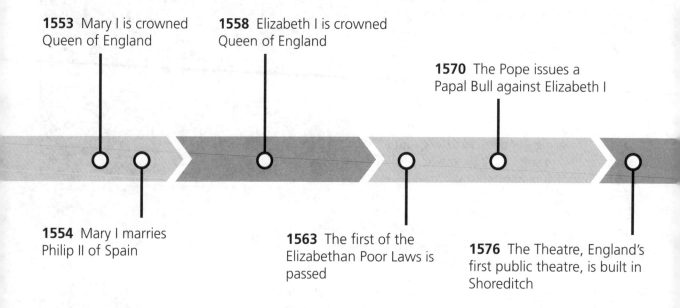

1553 Mary I is crowned Queen of England

1558 Elizabeth I is crowned Queen of England

1570 The Pope issues a Papal Bull against Elizabeth I

1554 Mary I marries Philip II of Spain

1563 The first of the Elizabethan Poor Laws is passed

1576 The Theatre, England's first public theatre, is built in Shoreditch

Key vocabulary

Armada Fleet of warships, often used to describe Spanish force sent to invade England in 1588

Babington Plot A foiled plot to kill Elizabeth I, which resulted in Mary Queen of Scots' execution

Burning at the stake A slow and painful execution, usually reserved for religious heretics

Counter-reformation Catholic fight back against the spread of Protestantism in Europe

Deserving poor Category developed by the Tudors for those amongst the poor in genuine need of help

Doublet and hose A buttoned up jacket and short padded trousers worn during the Tudor period

Elizabethan Religious Settlement A compromise agreement returning England to Protestantism but allowing Catholics to worship in secret

Foxe's Book of Martyrs A work of Protestant propaganda against Mary I, published in 1563

Galleon A large sailing ship, particularly from Spain

Gentleman Someone who earns enough money from land and investments not to work for a living

Gentry Class of wealthy landowners without noble titles, positioned just below the nobility

Gloriana A name given to Elizabeth towards the end of her reign, from the Latin for 'glorious'

Golden Age A period of flourishing in the history of a nation or an art form

Golden Hind Sir Francis Drake's ship, on which he completed his circumnavigation of the world

Hellburner A ship filled with explosives, set alight, abandoned and sailed towards the enemy

Martyr A person who is killed for their beliefs, often religious

New men Upwardly mobile men of the Tudor period, who benefitted from the weakening nobility

Papal Bull A formal and important announcement, issued by the Pope

Poor Laws Laws passed during the Tudor period, making local parishes raise money to help the poor

Privateer A private sailor or pirate, authorised by their government to attack enemy ships

Propaganda A piece of art or information used to promote a particular cause or point of view

Rack Torture device used slowly to stretch a person's body until all their joints dislocate

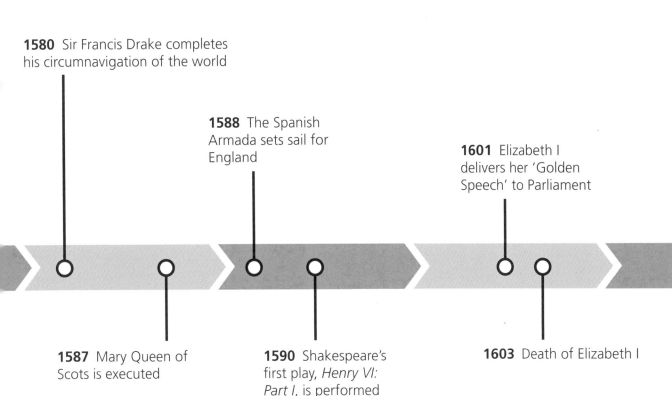

1580 Sir Francis Drake completes his circumnavigation of the world

1588 The Spanish Armada sets sail for England

1601 Elizabeth I delivers her 'Golden Speech' to Parliament

1587 Mary Queen of Scots is executed

1590 Shakespeare's first play, *Henry VI: Part I*, is performed

1603 Death of Elizabeth I

Key people

Duke of Medina Sidonia Commander of the Spanish Armada, who suffered from seasickness

Elizabeth I Queen from 1558 to 1603, and remembered as one of England's greatest monarchs

Francis Walsingham Principal Secretary and 'spymaster' to Elizabeth I

Lady Jane Grey Cousin of Edward VI, known as the 'nine day Queen' for her very brief reign

Mary I Queen who led England's counter-reformation, and earned the epithet 'Bloody'

Mary Queen of Scots Elizabeth I's Catholic cousin and the most significant threat to her reign

Philip II of Spain King of Spain, who for a time was the husband of Mary I and King of England

Francis Drake Sailor and privateer, and the first Englishman to circumnavigate the globe

Walter Raleigh English sailor and explorer, and a noted favourite of Queen Elizabeth I

William Shakespeare Celebrated English playwright who worked during the Tudor and Stuart periods

Key vocabulary

Royal Progress A summer journey taken by a monarch, visiting the stately homes of court favourites

Ruff An elaborate lace collar encircling the neck, fashionable during the Elizabethan period

Stately home A large country house at the centre of a gentleman or a noble's estate

Vagrant A person with no job, who travels from place to place begging

Wars of Religion A series of European wars fought between Protestants and Catholics from 1524 to 1648

Quiz questions

Chapter 1: Mary I's Counter-reformation

1. Which cousin of Edward VI was known as the 'nine day Queen'?
2. In what year was Mary I crowned Queen of England?
3. Who was Mary I's mother?
4. Which family member did Mary I imprison in the Tower of London after the 1554 Wyatt rebellion?
5. Which King of Spain was, for a short time, the husband of Mary I and King of England?
6. What do you call someone with beliefs that question the established church, such as Protestants during the reign of Mary I?
7. What slow and painful execution did Mary I use for punishing Protestants?
8. In total, how many Protestants did Mary I kill during her reign?
9. Which former Archbishop of Canterbury did Mary I execute?
10. What work of Protestant propaganda against Mary I was published in 1563?

Chapter 2: Elizabeth I

1. In what year was Elizabeth I crowned Queen of England?
2. What compromise agreement reached by Elizabeth I settled the future direction of the Church of England?
3. What rank of churchman did Elizabeth I keep as part of the Church of England?
4. What did the Pope issue against Elizabeth I in 1570?
5. Which of Elizabeth I's cousins posed the most significant threat to her reign?
6. Who was the Principal Secretary and 'spymaster' to Elizabeth I?
7. Which foiled plot to kill Elizabeth I resulted in her cousin's execution in 1587?
8. For what religious crime did Elizabeth I introduce the death penalty towards the end of her reign?
9. In all, how many Catholics were killed during Elizabeth's reign?
10. What popular torture device slowly stretched a person's body until all their joints dislocated?

Chapter 3: The Elizabethan Golden Age

1. What was the name of London's first public theatre, built in Shoreditch in 1576?
2. Which celebrated English playwright staged his first play in 1590?
3. How many plays did this celebrated English playwright write?
4. Which of Queen Elizabeth's favourites allowed her to use his cape to cross a puddle?
5. What pastime did this favourite of Queen Elizabeth's introduce to the royal court?
6. What were Queen Elizabeth's summer journeys to visit her court favourites called?
7. What Latin name was given to Elizabeth towards the end of her reign?
8. What do you call a private sailor or pirate, authorised by their government to attack enemy ships?
9. Who was the first Englishman to circumnavigate the globe?
10. What was the name of the ship on which he circumnavigated the globe?

Chapter 4: The Spanish Armada

1. In what year did the Spanish Armada set sail for England?
2. Which King of Spain ordered the Spanish Armada?
3. What event in 1587 seemed to guarantee a Protestant future for England, and prompted Spain to act?
4. How many galleons did the Spanish Armada contain?
5. Who was the commander of the Spanish Armada?
6. Where were the English moored when the Spanish missed their best chance of victory?
7. Why did the Spanish Armada sail to Calais before attacking the English?
8. What do you call the English ships that were filled with explosives, set alight, and sailed towards the Armada?
9. How many Spanish galleons were shipwrecked off the coast of Scotland and Ireland?
10. Where did Elizabeth I give her famous speech following the Battle of Gravelines?

Chapter 5: Rich and poor in Tudor England

1. How many noblemen were there in England by 1600?
2. Starting with the reign of Henry VII, what became illegal for noblemen to keep?
3. What class of wealthy landowners without noble titles were positioned just below the nobility?
4. Which upwardly mobile class during the Tudor period benefitted from the weakening nobility?
5. What popular Elizabethan outfit consisted of a buttoned up jacket and short padded trousers?
6. What elaborate lace collar, encircling the neck, was fashionable during the Elizabethan period?
7. The rapid growth of what during the 16th century made unemployment common?
8. What term was used to describe a person with no job, who travelled from place to place begging?
9. How would able-bodied people caught begging be punished?
10. What laws passed from 1563 onwards required local parishes to raise money for those in need?

William Collins' dream of knowledge for all began with the publication of his first book in 1819. A self-educated mill worker, he not only enriched millions of lives, but also founded a flourishing publishing house. Today, staying true to this spirit, Collins books are packed with inspiration, innovation and practical expertise. They place you at the centre of a world of possibility and give you exactly what you need to explore it.

Collins. Freedom to teach

Published by Collins
An imprint of HarperCollins*Publishers*
The News Building
1 London Bridge Street
London SE1 9GF

10 9 8 7 6 5 4 3 2 1

ISBN 978-0-00-819533-5

Publisher: Katie Sergeant
Editor: Hannah Dove
Author: Robert Peal
Fact-checker: Barbara Hibbert
Copy-editor: Sally Clifford
Image researcher: Alison Prior
Proof-reader: Ros and Chris Davies
Cover designer: Angela English
Cover image: © Victoria and Albert Museum, London
Production controller: Rachel Weaver
Typesetter: QBS
Printed and bound by Martins, UK

Acknowledgments

Every effort has been made to trace copyright holders and to obtain their permission for the use of copyright material. The publishers will gladly receive any information enabling them to rectify any error or omission at the first opportunity. The publishers would like to thank the following for permission to reproduce copyright material:

(t = top, b = bottom, c = centre, l = left, r = right)

Cover & p1 © Victoria and Albert Museum, London; p2t Ian G Dagnall/Alamy; p2b Heritage Image Partnership Ltd/ Alamy; p3t The burning of William Sawtre, illustration from 'Acts and Monuments' by John Foxe, ninth edition, pub. 1684 (litho), English School, (17th century)/Private Collection/The Stapleton Collection/Bridgeman Images; p3b Granger Historical Picture Archve/Alamy; p4t World History Archive/Alamy; p4b Ian Dagnall/Alamy; p5r Steve Sant/Alamy; p5l Ian Dagnall/Alamy; p6t Stocksnapper/Shutterstock; p6b World History Archive/Alamy; p7t Queen Elizabeth I in procession with her Courtiers (c.1600/03) from 'Memoirs of the Court of Queen Elizabeth' after an oil attributed to Robert Peake (c.1592–1667) at Sherborne Castle, published in 1825 (w/c and gouache on paper), Essex, Sarah Countess of (d.1838)/Private Collection/The Stapleton Collection/Bridgeman Images; p7b LOOK Die Bildagentur der Fotografen GmbH/Alamy; p8 World History Archive/Alamy; p9 National Geographic Creative/ Alamy; p10t A Fête at Bermondsey, c.1570 (oil on panel), Gheeraerts, Marcus, the Elder (c.1520–90)/Hatfield House, Hertfordshire, UK/Bridgeman Images; p10b ACTIVE MUSEUM/Alamy; p11 Fotosearch/Stringer/Getty

Collins

Key Stage 3
Early Modern Britain
The later Tudors

The Knowing History unit booklets help you to:

- Think critically about the past by focusing on the knowledge you need and then checking your understanding.

- Learn history through extraordinary people, amazing facts, and a distinctly engaging narrative.

- Remember key dates, vocabulary and significant people with the 'Knowledge organiser'.

- Test your knowledge with 'Quiz questions' for each chapter.

Knowing History Early Modern Britain booklets

Henry VIII and the Reformation   978-0-00-819532-8
The age of encounters   978-0-00-819536-6
The later Tudors   978-0-00-819533-5
The English Civil War   978-0-00-819534-2
Commonwealth and Restoration   978-0-00-819535-9
Georgian Britain   978-0-00-819537-3

The Early Modern Britain booklets are also available in:
Early Modern Britain 1509–1760 Student Book 2

Medieval Britain
410–1509
Student Book 1
978-0-00-819523-6

Early Modern Britain
1509–1760
Student Book 2
978-0-00-819524-3

Modern Britain
1760–1900
Student Book 3
978-0-00-819525-0

Free Teacher Guides available on www.collins.co.uk

Collins
FREEDOM TO TEACH

Find us at **www.collins.co.uk**
and follow our blog – articles and
information by teachers for teachers.
🐦 @FreedomToTeach

ISBN 978-0-00-819533-5

9 780008 195335 >